AF316942

THE MANUSCRIPT

The Manuscript

CASSANDRA P. ROBINS

IngramSpark

CONTENTS

~ 16 ~
Clara Bow
29

~ 17 ~
The Manuscript
30

Now It's Yours

Dedication

"I hope you know what you've meant to me.
One day I hope we're all happy.
Thank you for coming to my show.
First my story, then I must go.
See you there, in the pages within.
Here hold my hand, dearest friend."

~C.P.R.

~ 1 ~

FORTNIGHT

The touch of your skin as you ran your hand up my thigh.
The feeling of forever, the look in your eye.

A whirlwind of emotions that swept us away.
It was only a fortnight which you'd stay.

They took you from me, the savage beasts.
Seeking the soul within me for their many feasts.

Chaining me up, while pinning me down.
Their hands around my throat, as I lie on the ground.

A single tear, I allowed to fall.
Cursing their names, I'd fool them all.

It was those who once loved me, that have shown me what a
dragon truly is.
Couldn't they see... all I wanted was to be his...

Why couldn't they see...
I was left broken and lonely...

Why couldn't they see...
You were the one for me...

~ 2 ~

THE TORTURED POETS
DEPARTMENT

Swinging from vines, caged and confined.
I'd recess to the tortured poet's department deep within my
own mind.

Walls of drawers, my memories held.
Records of success, and the things I've failed.

I sit at my desk, facing yours.
Ignoring the pain seeping from my pores.

I insert a page into the typewriter you left.
As you were taken from me in the theft.

What was once a home, now empty stripped bare to the bone.
The wind blowing through the broken windows now that you're
gone.

My fingers begin gliding across the keys.
A letter to the vipers begging please.

For just a moment more with you.

You truly were one of the few.

Who ever saw me for who I was.
Tame like a lion, swift as a dove.

It's in the tortured poet's department,
where I still feel your love wrapped around me like a warm
embrace.
I close my eyes seeing your face.

You're sitting across from me, in the chair that was yours.
With the wound still bleeding, I fall down on all fours.

Crying out to the sky, screaming to die.
Couldn't they see me, why did they choose to despise.

The only one who'd been there all along.
They had no idea you were the muse to almost every song.

Thats been written with you on my mind.
It's within your heart that I find.

True solace, courage, and love.
They shot down my angel sent from above.

Don't worry though darling, you'll always reside.
In the tortured poet's department where I'll recess and hide.

~ 3 ~

MY BOY ONLY BREAKS HIS
FAVORITE TOYS

They said I was plastic, that I couldn't move.
I knew in my heart, I still had so much to prove.

They say they love me, the crowd goes wild.
Yet the soul inside you remains a child.

You see, my boy only breaks his favorite toys.
Taking for granted in life, the things which bring joys.

Wholesome yet beautiful, I thought I was sure.
You'd been the prince to my kingdom, the one with the cure.

You swept me up, while I was new.
Then the shine wore off, as the scars shown through.

You cast me aside, into a pile.
I sat there and cried, only for a while.

It wasn't long before the chamber maids came.
Detailing in whispers of a new dame.

Which you'd found a while back.
That's when I felt it, the plastic began to crack.

It wasn't long before I was completely broken.
The memories of us, the only token.

I'd take with me into the bin.
Ever longing to be put back together again.

~ 4 ~

DOWN BAD

I'd been down before, haven't we all?
Yet this time there was no one to call.

I'd been locked away in this tower of gold.
My earthly belongings long ago sold.

I've sat at this window, watching life pass me by.
It had been so long now, I've forgotten how to cry.

I'm only freed to put on a show.
Three hours of me and then you'd all go.

Back to your lives as if nothing changed.
Unknowing I'd stare into your windows somewhat deranged.

Secretly wishing for someone to see.
The human beneath the celebrity.

So many years have passed me by.
I'm now down bad longing to die.

Stripped naked of basic needs.

Crowds screaming more as I'm down on my knees.

How can I show them there's depth beneath my wings.
I continue holding my breath seeing what the day brings.

The thing is the days without a show.
There is no light coming through my window.

Cast out into darkness with no light.
No safe place to harness, no end in sight.

Yeah, I'm down bad, worse than I've known.
If I hadn't let them in, would he have gone?

~ 5 ~

SO LONG, LONDON

Trains charging through winter rains.
Drops sliding down windowpanes.

When in Rome do as the Roman's do.
Yet for London so long to you.

So long, London it's been fun.
I hate to leave, but I have to run.

There's nothing left for me here.
I've faced my death through hell and fear.

So long, London I've come and gone.
I've left the queen there on her throne.

No longer writing down by the lakes.
Nor the Woodvale Forest full of snakes.

So long, London I'll hold you dear.
There's nothing left for me here.

So long, London you meant so much.

I'll never forget the feel of your touch.

Elegance at teatime never fades.
Instead of aces I kept coming up spades.

~ 6 ~

BUT DADDY I LOVE HIM

Dear reader, I start off this letter to you today.
With something I've so long needed to say.

I met a man backstage at my show.
I guess it was about ten years ago.

In the instance that our eyes met.
I felt a feeling I hadn't yet.

It lit a fire deep within my soul.
I knew I couldn't let this one go.

I snuck in through his garden every night that I could.
Knowing I couldn't tell of him and if I should.

I'd allow in the snakes, those who wanted me dead.
Standing up to my father this is what I said.

But daddy I love him, this man of the hour.
Allow me to see him, it's within your power.

Please don't lock me in that tower so high.

If you do daddy, I'll wither and die.

Allow me to see him just one more time.
Please let me see him, that man is mine.

~ 7 ~

FRESH OUT THE SLAMMER

Fresh out the slammer, free at last.
Left to pick up the pieces of my broken past.

Fresh out the slammer, feeling the sun.
No longer feeling a need to run.

Paid for my crimes, six long years.
Facing the dragons, conquering all fears.

Fresh out the slammer, into the night.
Breathing fresh air underneath the moonlight.

Fresh out the slammer, I've longed for the day.
I'd set down my pen, nothing left to say.

Fresh out the slammer, I left you there.
You're no longer a burden I have to bear.

Fresh out the slammer, time to have fun.
If you were to see me, darling I'd run.

~ 8 ~

FLORIDA

Descending the steps of the plane.
A drop on my shirt, was it a tear or rain?

Florida, how long has been?
With your pale beaches marked by men.

Grains of sand like an hourglass.
Each one reminding me of the recent past.

So much happened on that plane.
Nothing will ever be the same.

A life imagined, lost to the wind.
Will my heart ever beat again?

CPR unable to save me.
As our ship was lost out to sea.

The only passenger now is me.
Me...

Florida, how have you been

It's been awhile now my friend

Lost to a cage where I split into three.
While taking a look back, recreating parts of me.

~ 9 ~

GUILTY AS SIN

Caught, cuffed, and jailed.
You see for me, that ship had sailed.

I met you down in a crowded cafe.
Upon first sight I was mesmerized I must say.

The way your hair curled by your eye.
I knew then, you were the guy.

I'd spend my nights dreaming of.
The one who was sent, just for me from above.

We met in secret for so long.
You were the muse to almost every song.

That I'd write in the many years.
Unable to be together due to our fears.

If they found out, what would they say?
We tried that once; they marked the day.

On their calendars as the day, I'd be taken in.

The crime, loving you, me? Guilty as sin.

Passing all these houses I'd never be invited in.
Tell me, how am I innocent, yet proven guilty as sin.

~ 10 ~

WHO'S AFRAID OF LITTLE
OLD ME

Thunder and lightning as I speak.
Who's afraid of little old me?

Rain clouds forming above your head.
Just say if you wish me dead.

Breaking free from the chains.
That once held me down.

Foregoing all pain.
Seeking revenge on the town.

Who called me wicked, and threw me out.
Now it's my turn to go about.

Making sure the truth is known.
Yet now that I'm back, you all are gone.

Who's afraid of little old me?
Everyone apparently.

~ 11 ~

I CAN FIX HIM (NO REALLY I CAN)

.

I can fix him, no really I can.
Through the fire that is my man.

I see a side you've only dreamed.
He's far less guilty than he seemed.

Yet the vipers hissed every time we kissed.
The love of my life, a chance I missed.

I'll never find what I found in him.
I'll never feel that way again.

Trust me I can fix him, no really I can.
Why can't they believe me, shot down where I stand.

I'd give up this life, and all I've earned.
I'd stand by and watch as it all burned.

Just to have a chance with him.
Why did I ever tell you of him...

Now he's gone unable to deal.
It was you who made him feel.

That this life with me by his side.
Would only be possible if we chose to hide.

That was a life he wasn't willing to live.
As you continue to take all I've had to give.

I've given you all every ounce of myself.
Placing my wants neatly on a shelf.

So that maybe the crowd will cheer.
He had to go, due to the fear.

I'd never truly be happy without the fans.
Now it's just me here, alone again.

~ 12 ~

LOML

I found something once I can only describe.
As a feeling I've not since been able to find.

I knew what to call it before I told you.
The love of my life left lonely and blue.

The love of my life, that's what you were.
I was the misses to your sir.

Hidden away, deep into the night.
No one saw us by the moonlight.

Until these feelings, I couldn't hide anymore.
I knew you loved me, but you weren't as sure.

That the vipers would stay at bay.
I never saw it coming, they wouldn't let you stay.

I gave it all, just to lose.
The love of my life, the only one whose.

Ever saw me for who I am.

I committed to you, I was going to take the stand.

Telling the jury, you weren't that bad.
You knew they wouldn't believe me, no matter what evidence I had.

So I enter in all of my files.
Still our see you soons, became sometime after whiles.

The distance grew further, as the nights grew cold.
Waking one day to ourselves old.

We'd longed for so long to be as one.
How was I to know that you'd become.

The loss of my life, the only one I'd choose.
Yet the vipers chose for me, causing me to lose.

The only one, who I ever truly loved.
Perhaps we'll be together in another life, my love.

~ 13 ~

I CAN DO IT WITH A BROKEN HEART

Lying on the floor of my dressing room.
Knowing the show would start all too soon.

Unable to move, they called out my name.
Yet my thoughts were of you, even done so in vain.

Unable to process the hurt over the cheers.
After all they'd been with me all these years.

How could I lay here letting them down.
Some had traveled so far to this town.

Where we met for the show that night.
They were expecting a version of me who was still alive.

What they didn't know was I was already shot on sight.
The wound still bleeding all throughout the night.

Yet I rose from the floor where I laid.
I knew I could do it, after all I had paid.

To the demons who lived in my head.
After all it wasn't the fans who wanted me dead.

So I went out there, and put on a show.
Yet after it was over, you all had to go.

If only you knew the pain I'd gone through.
Yet I would never have bothered any of you.

With any of that, it was my cross to bear.
After all I can do it with a broken heart, I was already there.

Long before any of you had came.
Living in misery somewhat insane.

Yet never allowing a single tear to fall.
If I had, I would have lost it all.

You would have been there for me, that I know.
Yet admitting it was over, that we had to go.

It was something far greater than I could stand.
How did I become that girl, so taken by a man.

I'd given the best parts of myself too.
Yet here I was broken, left lonely and blue.

Tell me dear reader, have you felt this pain?
If so meet me by the tower in the midnight rain.

I say aloud I can do it with a broken heart.
Standing there behind the curtain waiting for the show to start.

~ 14 ~

THE SMALLEST MAN WHO EVER LIVED

By the time I met you I had already given all I had to give.
To the smallest man who ever lived.

You see he had saved me, from that tower of gold.
Where I was locked away waiting for my story to unfold.

It was those who loved me, that had locked me up high.
In that cage up in the sky.

Begging I sing, dance, and entertain.
They never once realized it was my tears falling, not rain.

With a smile on my face, I gave them what they asked.
Never realizing the magnitude of the task.

I played for hours, until my fingers bled.
I gave all I had to stay out of my own head.

Where I was burdened to face the pain.
Praying I'd never see the smallest man who ever lived again.

Though he had once saved me.
I was in his debt, something he never let me forget.

I knew that one day I'd finally break free.
Then I would finally get to be me.

The human beneath the celebrity.
The one only he was allowed to see.

~ 15 ~

THE ALCHEMY

I showed you a part of me.
I'd never allowed anyone else to see.

I kept it hidden so that it was mine.
I so long hoped that no one would find.

My little haven inside of myself.
I kept it placed neatly up on a shelf.

Deep within my heart and soul.
Keeping my freedom, the only goal.

It wasn't until I met you, that I would see.
Outside of myself into your alchemy.

It was contagious, the way you were free.
No chains that bind, unlike me.

I'd never known the life you live.
If only I didn't have one fuck to give.

Then maybe I'd be free too.

For now it's your alchemy that's getting me through.

I use to see a world full of color, now it's all blue.
Yet when I'm with you, there's this vibrant hue.

Bright, and warm like bathing in the sun.
Miles of beaches, just for us to run.

No cameras flashing, into the night.
No reason to fear, not one single fright.

Your heart, it glowed throughout your being.
You're now the muse of the songs I'll be singing.

I hope you know, just how you glow.
I hope to see you there, at my show.

~ 16 ~

CLARA BOW

The films were silent, the voices in my head were loud.
As I stood there smiling in front of the crowd.

Cameras flashing like a sea of stars.
Do they even know me, or where they are?

I guess they think I'm some modern Clara Bow.
Inviting them in to another show.

Yet, they're never welcome, the ones who haunt.
Where's my knight in shining, so galant.

Then I remember I have to save myself.
This isn't the twenties when the endings were happy.
I wasn't the Daisy to some modern day Gatsby.

Nor was I Clara Bow, If I had been would you still go?
Leaving me there, without the faintest of glow.
Wandering aimlessly out in the snow.

~ 17 ~

THE MANUSCRIPT

So you've found me, my hidden gem.
I've put this out so that if you were him.

You would know how I truly felt.
When you touched me, I'd surely melt.

Into a puddle of love on the floor.
Pleading, begging, screaming for more.

So I hereby stand to plead my case.
Dreaming you'll find me again one day.

I never meant, for the venom to spread.
If only it had been me they wanted dead.

All these things, I keep inside.
To stay safe, I have to hide.

From the archers and their bows.
Buying time, by booking shows.

I've left it all here on the page.

Consider this outpour of female rage.

The manuscript which I've lived.
I'll never forget, yet will I forgive?

I guess we'll all have to wait and see.
Just how much more is taken from me.

For now I've given, all I have to give.
Here, the manuscript of how I've lived.

Now It's Yours

Now that I've given my story, it's your turn.
Use the following pages to write out the story of your dreams.
Never forgetting, there isn't one rose garden free from thorns.

-C.P.R.

THE END